LOOK AT YOU!

LOOK AT YOU!

LOOK AT YOU!

DO YOU LIKE WHAT YOU SEE?

Yasmin Y. Pacheco M.

authorHOUSE®

AuthorHouse™
1663 Liberty Drive
Bloomington, IN 47403
www.authorhouse.com
Phone: 1-800-839-8640

Published by AuthorHouse 01/08/2015

ISBN: 978-1-4969-6074-0 (sc)
ISBN: 978-1-4969-6073-3 (e)

Library of Congress Control Number: 2014922593

Saint Francis of Assisi prayer

Lord, make me an instrument of Your peace;
Where there is hatred, let me sow love;
Where there is injury, pardon;
Where there is discord, harmony;
Where there is error, truth;
Where there is doubt, faith;
Where there is despair, hope;
Where there is darkness, light;
And where there is sadness, joy.
O Divine Master, Grant that I may not so much seek
To be consoled as to console;
To be understood as to understand;
To be loved as to love.
For it is in giving that we receive;
It is in pardoning that we are pardoned;
And it is in dying that we are born to eternal life.

With all my heart I want to thank and dedicate this book to:

God, Holy Spirit, Jesus, Mother Mary, Angels Divine, Angels of Light, Beloved Archangels, Ascended Masters and Holy Masters.

My beloved parents, Gustavo and Zoraida

My beloved son, Mi Peque, Gustavo Alejandro

My siblings, beloved sisters and brothers, nieces and nephews

My friends, my chosen family.

You all... Thanks

About the author

Woman, mother, daughter, sister, aunt, friend and warrior of universal energy. Committed to find that inner peace that allows her to be part of the world peace. In a process that takes several years with trial and errors, with ups and downs, her constant search that ends into a physical, psychic and spiritual transformations. Long journey, a long road runs and more to discover, with the certainty of doing what her heart guide her to, there is no error if you follow what the heart guides and with the goal of such consent to help you and everyone else.

She was born in Caracas Venezuela, in a big family with 8 siblings, she is the little one, she is smart, kind and sweet, since she was a child she enjoys dance all kind of music, she also enjoys listen to the music, read, write, meditate, healthy cook, stay in contact with the nature and with her family. She enjoys

 kundalini Yoga, she have been practicing for three year now, she likes all natural practices as chi Kung, tai chi and psycho physical gymnastics, she enjoys her quiet time as well. She is a Certified Angel Card Reader and Advance Angel Tarot and Oracle Card Reader by Doreen Virtue and Radleigh Valentine, She has a certification in Reiki Usui Tibetan ART III, she participated at the Kabbalah Centre in the power of Kabbalah 1 and 2. She heal herself form overweight, sadness, stress, with an inside work and with a transformation in her habits, sleep, foods, thoughts and deepen her connection with the divine light and the Angels.

You are perfect, Just the Way You Are

You're perfect just the way you are, with your skills and opportunities for improvement, you just have to accept and love yourself as you are, that way you will see another perspective in life, each person sees situations from their own unique perspective, is why sometimes is difficult for us to understand each other. Each one is inside her own, seeing everything in its way, it is interesting that occasionally get out and realize that we are all one, and that the master key that opens all doors within you, and is unlimited and infinite God or Light or as you like to call it, shared love with us, because we are all part of the same energy of God, in the same light... Do you believe it? Me neither, and the true is... WE ARE ALL ONE, AND LOVE IS THE GIFT THAT WE ALL HAVE.

I could cite countless books and authors who speak on this subject, however, I prefer to tell you to listen to your inner voice and ask for assistance to the angels of light, to guide you as to me and anyone who ask. Love and accept yourself as you are, perfect this is the key to happiness... To be at peace with yourself and with others... Ahhhh. Also wanted to say I do not take anything personal. Everyone has in their head their own situations... Breathe, smile and loves everyone, from the bottom of your heart and see how you feel some relief... And it changes your perspective on life.

Well actually there are many situations much growth I have experienced and many books I read eh... But as I said before each individual requires to live their own experiences to achieve their personal and spiritual growth. I would say it is easy but nothing is gained easily endures, it is important that you appreciate and thank every situation and see a blessing in each of them, do not forget to breathe and to smile though even if you don't want to... Ahhhh another important thing is to learn to differentiate between your inner voice and the voice of the ego, always loving your inner voice, not afraid, not judges, learn to control your thoughts, do not let your mind think for you, you are in charge of your life, or your existence I like this phrase. All you require was given to you, all the treasures are at the center of your heart, seek and find. Ask and you will get. Open your heart, love, forgive and live in the present, every second counts, every second you have a new chance to decide, to change you mind, to learn, to live... Relax, enjoy the better things in life are Free... Enjoy the singing of the birds, the flowers in the spring, heat and summer greenery, rain, drought. Enjoy everything, it all happens... Nothing is eternal, nothing will ever be the same and the past is past... The future does not exist. You build your actions present then.... You have the opportunity to create Your own experience every day and enjoy every moment as if it were your last. Total none of us knows when we'll leave, all we have is the now... Enjoy it. Do things that you like, dance, sing, write, read, play, run, screaming... Whatever makes you happy is fine. Whenever you do with all your heart and with infinite love.

Wao... Much information? Okay... Get into it, take what you find useful, share, enjoy and just for today Love yourself! With all your heart. Accept yourself just the way you are and accept others as they are, you will see how is your day happier.

Only you know what is good for you, only you know what your mission is, only you can find out, you have all the tools you need, and yes, in your heart. Mute your thoughts and give room for your inner voice. There you will find all the answers to your questions and all the instructions you require. Within you. No one else can take charge of your existence. Only you. One step at a time, one day at a time, one second at a time, deep breathe, smiles and moves on. At your own rhythm. Each one has its own rhythm... Just go ahead and find yours, know, learn about yourself. What do you like? What you do not like? Why do not like? They try again, or your impressions are learned from someone else or what is said to be good or not? Relearn, retraces, try again or find new situations that really identify with your inner self, with yourself. Listen to yourself, listen to your body, take care of yourself, physically and spiritually, what you eat, what you read, what you think, choose only what you nourish you.

What ever makes you feel good with yourself.
Remember... Only you know it

Perhaps this spinning on the same subject,
you may need a little time to tune your ears to your
inner voice, bear remember that your inner voice is
only love. If not that what you hear or feel fear, then
the speaker is the ego. From love all the choices you
make will make you happier each day. Remember....
Breathe, smile and move on. Any tool that you
consider appropriate will be, take what you need,
applied and move on. Just like that as an obstacle.
Or a game with levels when you exceed a level, opens
another and so on. It's like a rally, you find a track
and you reveal the next instructions to follow. It
is wonderful... The timing is perfect. Just like the
synchronicity of the Universe. Everything is perfect
as it is! You too. Have no doubt about it.

Never too late to start. All in good time. And my
favorite phrase. God's time is infinite and perfect.

In addition you will always will have doubts, if it
is the right way or if you're doing well, and let me tell
you that all paths are correct and always everything
will be fine, you always have the opportunity to
choose again and take a new path. You can try

 all ways, all come to the light, your essence is the same as that of light, because we are made in his image and likeness. what do you think about it?? Incredible. Truth? that is true! Don't worry. Me neither believed it. Slowly, step by step, slowly but surely. Everyone has their own truth, each person is unique and irreplaceable, each person has a gift to share and develop, find yours, and yes, is within you, no matter where you are told that all the hidden treasures, muted voices and noises external and internal concentrate in that loving and accurate voice that is speaking to you and guiding you. I'm not going to say it's easy, but yes I'm going to say it's not impossible, anything is possible.

Gratitude and forgiveness

To me have been the keys to remove that extra weight back, I thank you for absolutely everything in my life, although at the time it doesn't sound like the best for you, you will soon realize that it was all a blessing, only seeks clarity to accept and enjoy all situations, learning... Forgiveness... Mmmmm Big words, not easy to understand or implement. The first person you need to forgive is yourself. Yes yourself... By judging negatively, being unfair with you to please others before yourself. That takes focus and love. Forgive yourself and others, you'll see a new episode will begin in your life. I know it's not easy, but I assure you it is not impossible. Give thanks and forgive. Liberate so many self-imposed judgments... So many self-imposed limitations... So many auto beliefs imposed and enforced by others... Validate all... Check it is good for you if it's worth, if it makes you happy.... If not discard it. Create your own beliefs, routines after all every one is perfect in its own way and if everyone is unique why we would have an equal standard for all? Do not be labeled or Tags... That's not nice. The more spontaneous you are, the more you'll enjoy the small and almost imperceptible things that gives us everyday, like birds singing and sometimes delights us and we are so "busy" being unhappy that neither hear. The most beautiful things in life are simple, easy and perfect... just need to be alert in the here and now and enjoying every moment. No expectations... Although not without intention.

Again, focus, listen, love yourself. You're perfect and beloved, as you are, you're UNIQUE. Enjoy it.

When you learn to appreciate and be thankful you have many more doors open to achieve your desires. Regardless of the situation presented to you thanks and praise is for sure make you feel that everything is and will be better than good for you. Using an expression that I love and it seems shocking to the ears of others is I'm extremely well. Everything is wonderful in my life. It seems to dislike to know that you're happy or good things happen to you and my best antidote is to share my joy with others, enlighten others, do not let your light goes for comments or unpleasant feelings that others perceive. Really only you have control of your life and no one but you can make you be sad or depressed. Remember that what others think is THEIR truth and not yours. So... focus on your spiritual growth and walk with firm steps towards the light. Lifting them after every setback and keeping your heart happy and your mind with positive thoughts. The truth it's easy, and it costs a bit at first. Little by little it is achieving. One step at a time. The important thing is to keep your focus on your heart no matter what, that does not mean you isolate yourself, no, nothing like that, the more you share with others is becoming easier. Your thoughts must be pure and loving. All in love is achievable, EVERYTHING. Take care of your body, guard your mind, your thoughts and feelings. You decide what you want or not to manifest. Everything was given. You just have to remember and act accordingly. There are so many things... More yet all are the same. So what will focus on your inner work and everything else will just be fine.

When you fell tormented by thoughts or feelings, repeating a mantra, a prayer, something that connects you with your higher self and breath do not stop breathing, you can also seek help from higher beings, Angels of light, Archangels, Ascended Masters or any spiritual figure that is your preference. They will be pleased to help you stay in peace and find options to move forward with love and joy. Everything is possible and viable. Just be certain that if it is mean to be it will manifests in your life. The beauty of life is indescribable, its subtlety, its perfection... Wao. We just have to believe, to remember, to apply for and appreciated.

When you begin to awaken, you understand many things, things that I've learned is that nobody has power over you, only you decide who may be able to overshadow your light, sulk and even sad, yet that is a process in which, you must first know that nothing is personal, maybe that person is going through a bad time and unconsciously or conscious wants your attention, the best way to keep your light is knowing that it is not personal, that has nothing about you and your peace is not negotiable, offer help is a good option, ask the angels and archangels help for the person and know that everything happens for a reason and that in due course, appreciate the experience that allowed us to grow. Sometimes we have the evidence remix... That is repeated several times to see themselves learned and increasingly subtle type shell handle to see whether we fall again... Sometimes we fall, but as we go awakening and becoming aware of the wonderful universe that we have and how it works, every time we fall less and as we continue not playing the testing situation. It's easy, just takes time to wake up. Again the duo love-fear, always choose love, always always... And choose love... So always go for insurance on the way home...

Sometimes people will say you're crazy, you're weird, that if this or that... It happens all the time... I feel good with who I am. I used to live just to please everyone around me and believe me I was very unhappy, I felt depressed, lonely, anxious, because it was important what others think, now the most important thing is to feel good about myself and this is manifested as a great peace, better health, less stress and greater certainty that with love anything is possible, but the self is the first thing to grow, to love ourselves as we are is the key.

Maybe you don't understand much of what I'm talking about, but only read and take what fits your reality, listen to your inner voice, take control of your thoughts, words and actions. In sync internally and connect with the source of life and light that is within you, then you will get everything you are looking for, for you. There is no other place to look, there are actually many where to look, but where you are getting what you need is inside of you.

In my personal experience, I can tell you that truly difficult situations made me grow and taught me to value, appreciate the little things in life, to be at peace with myself and understand that everything that happens, happens for a reason and that perhaps in when you seem unfair, horrible and very strong, but the realities are small tests to help you find your way to peace, joy, self acceptance and understanding that everything happens and when it happens understand what was their reason for being. What I can tell you that worked in my cases was to learn how to silence the voice of the ego, which criticizes and judges and learn to listen to your true inner voice is sweet and loving and has all calculated to make you happy every moment of your life.

I can also tell you that when you start the inner work of self healing, automatically as it like pieces of a puzzle all the other pieces in your life begin to fit, you start to see things from a different perspective, from love and not from fear and miraculously begin to listen, to listen to your body and cover their needs with love, you adjust your routines, you begin to take better care, to feed better, to find people who support you and help you with the next steps you start give in this new direction, you begin to incorporate new things in your life, at all levels, meditation better nutrition, exercise, kindest with yourself and with others thoughts. Although it sounds romantic start to see life lovely.

I can also tell you that is my personal opinion according to how I'm living my awakening of consciousness, however also say to you that every human being is unique and as such the process for each person is different. As they say, each head is a world... It also is, do not worry too much, give attendance to take a step at a time and keep constant there, without fail, because at first all change is challenging, gradually, incorporate activities that you are enjoying and in that time you fly by, and gradually see eliminate those that generate you anguish and despair. Gradually changing your environment and your routines you will feel better and better.

Woao. Life is so simple... And beautiful. Just see the nature and celebrate the graceful to be part of It. Part of God, the light, the energy whatever you believe in... So. Connect with your inner guide and be one within. All you want, need or desire you got it already. Just believe, come through your dreams... Be one with yourself and serve, help others, in small things. It doesn't matter... Just help, serve, love and be one with your inner self, with the God within you, share the light, be the light... Live the present time, enjoy it. All the answers are within you, with you. Ask and you will get. You have to remember that you are a beloved child of God. And be sure of that. Trust and you will see, the blessings in all the things that surround you, every step you take, every heartbeat, every breath you take is a blessing. Be thankful and the grace of God will show you the real life, the reality of our life, of our soul, the joy of been.

Sometimes it's not easy, sometimes you'll feel lonely, sad, and tired, but this is another test for you, to make you stronger, vulnerable, and to fight the ego, the ego wants you to be small and dark but God wants you to be infinite and lighten. You just need to have faith, and continue your path, with love, peace, serenity and giving you the permission to be weak sometimes, to make mistakes sometimes, and to learn about it, who you are? And how you feel, without guilt, we are perfect, everybody is... We are beloved child's of God, enjoy the path, this is the live, this is your gift. Live your life with self-love and compassion and share it with everyone you get in touch with. Keep doing baby steps on the road and learning everyday how to stay happy and healthy. Your body is going to recognize your God within and will give you messages about what kind of foods, thoughts, feelings and insides jobs you have to develop every day. Trust, surrender, let God guide your life, listen to your inner voice, follow your inner guidance, ask for help anytime you need it, and you will have it. We are special and beloved Child's of God and he never let us down. Every day is a new opportunity to begin again, release de fear, forgives everyone but yourself and call upon God and the messengers for help. You will be more than fine.

Believe it. You don't have to force anything, let things be and be you, the unique and perfect creation of God's love, enjoy being you, knowing who you really are and what you like or not, without external conditioning, just BE. And enjoy what you see without judgment, with kindness and self-love. You will realize that you don't even know who you are, and what your deep desires are, but step by step you will figure it out. Be patience don't blame you or others all the answer are inside of you, just listen, slow down, be grateful and if you don't like what you see, be grateful anyway there is a reason for all things that happens.

Do all things from you heart and you will never fail, you can't be wrong, well there are not such things as right or wrong is only anyone perspective. You will know about it. Just do things than make you feel good, happy and beloved, and you will be bless with the development of you unique gift. You will realize that this is the most important thing in your life and then you will know that it doesn't matter what the others think about you is only their own perspective, and have nothing to do with you, but the real important thing is Your own acceptance of yourself been and doing. Without guilt or hard feelings to others and with compassion for other but yourself.

This is a personal workout, but not only physical one, is more internal, spiritual, build and heal yourself from the inside and the outside will change. As I said, is not going to be easy but is not impossible, keep doing your daily job and You will have the guidance to move forward, don't give up.

The day begins with grateful for been alive, and calling upon God, Holy Spirit, Jesus, mother Mary, Angels, Archangels, or whoever you believe in, the important thing is say thanks, thanks, thanks, in the beginning and in the end of all days. Ask for help, guidance, light, compassion and whatever you want to realize in you day, be open minded and listen to you inner voice. Each day is going to be better than the others. Keep positive thoughts and accept you negative toughs don't denied it, because becomes stronger. Just be aware that they exist and replace them with positive thoughts. Then let them go. They will come back, and them again replace it with positive thoughts, keep your mind on guard, and step by step you will take control of it, You'll become alert and positive.

You also must purify your incomes, like TV programs, videos, negative peoples, etc. I mean try to connect with the beautiful part of everything, avoid bad news in newspapers and TV news, violent programs and videos, and people who only talk negative or violent things, because this things conscious or unconscious will affect you energy slowing it down, connect with the nature, as much as you can, listen to the birds in the morning, enjoy the sun rising and the sunset, the moon, the stars, enjoy every single beautiful things that we have, walk with you head up not watching the ground, look the horizon always, and your live is gone change for good. I know that it seems difficult but is not, if I did it you can do it too, you just have to make a commitment with yourself an honor it, be patient and be kind with yourself and others, don't judge, remember each human being have their own perspective so you too, just relax and send energy of love to anything or anyone that disturb you and be sure that it's going to pass too... All things are temporary, we all change every day, our body change, our mind and souls changes, we are not the same as yesterday, every day you have the opportunity to begin again, to make new decisions to be happier and healthier than the day before, don't lose this magic opportunity, do small things all days and more small things the other day an so it is. Like I said before, baby steps all days.

Another thing that was important to me was liberate myself from the expectations form other people, the vulnerability, tuff thing, It doesn't matter what the others think or said about you, the real thing that matters is what you think o said about you, this is a big deal, don't expect approval from the outside, just do all things with love in your heart and everything is going to be fine, don't harm yourself with criticism or judgment, we make mistakes, and we learn about it, and try again in the different way, until we make it, forgive yourself and other every day and move forward. Feel any emotion of the moment accept it, work with it take the good part of it inhale, exhale and let it go, learn your lesson an move on, don't stuck yourself in lamentation or bad judgments of yourself or others, is not necessary and is not going to help in your path, you need to go ahead, another day is coming soon, don't lose your precious time with negative things, ask for help if you need, and you will get it, for sure, be nice and smile, no matter what... You will see beautiful changes in your life and all around you, is just a new habit to incorporate in you daily life, like brush your teeth in the morning as soon as you get up, do it all days and do it with love in your heart no matter what's happens keep it on mind, smile, breath and be nice with yourself and others. Sooner or later you will begin to feel better each day and you will see changes in all aspects of your live, keep it on mind, is a work of all days without a break, there's not holidays in your spiritual path, do it and do it as soon as possible it will be an amazing path to joy.

Do every day one thing that makes you happy and one more. You will remember your passion, your vocation, what you want to do and how you will do it. All the tools you need are already inside of you, just listen you inner voice is a lovely low voice who talks to you every day and every time, giving you lovely advices to accomplish your tasks in a better way possible for you higher self. So it is. I really know that you think that everything I'm telling you is impossible, I thought it too, but I did it, so you can do it too. As I said before, the beginning is going to be maybe a little hard, because your ego is going to tell you that you are crazy, and it's not going to work and it's ridiculous, and everything, and this is the proof that you are in your path. Then you have to keep going and you will begin to listen you inner voice every day a little more and silence your ego a little more, don't give up. And begin NOW. Baby steps that's it.

Well... Let see how I can explain this... A beautiful day, sun is shining, birds are singing, sky is clear blue with some Angel clouds, flowers everywhere...this could be your morning too, you just have to decide to see, the small gifts that every day brings to us. Be present, be aware, I have to tell you that at the beginning, you will not enjoy it, it seems simple, but later on you will love it as I do. When I wake up this morning sleepy I have two choices, stay in bed and wake up later, in a hurry and in a bad mood, or wake up early do my meditation, do some exercise, take a bath and a delicious breakfast. I made my decision and the universe conspire with me to do the rest of my day nice and peaceful. You have the choice every day, to do a small unlike thing that brings you great results or to do the ease things than keep you stressful and mad. Everything in this live is about decisions, and you can change yours any time you want to, if something make you unhappy, just release it from your live, let it go, and do it in another way. You will see a lot of changes in your life, you need to be conscious of your own life, you have to be present, and make your own decisions and take the control of your life or let the life take control of you. Easy... Not so much at the beginning, but with patience and love you will get it. If you go back into your old habits for a while it's fine, don't give up, forgive you and move on, try it again and again, it's you live, you deserve the opportunity to stay in peace, happy and abundant in your live path. If you don't have the inspiration to do something at the moment, is fine, do something else, you will know what to do or not to do, just listening to your mind, keeping it quiet, feeling you emotions, keeping it lovely, and being grateful, with anything that happens, no matter what, you'll say thanks, and realize that there is a ultimate purpose in any situation in your live, for good and for better... Everything is happening in the perfect timing, to accomplish your higher self-path. Sooner or later you will realize that, and you will laugh of it.

First of all you need to learn how to be happy with yourself. Self-acceptation, self-love, self-forgiveness, you have to learn how to be alone with yourself, to know yourself, be quiet, alone, enjoy the loneliness, be your best friend, take care of yourself that's the only way to do these all things with someone else. If you don't know yourself you can't show anyone else who you are because you don't know, you can't love anyone else, because you don't love yourself, and so it's. Don't be afraid to be alone, don't be afraid to make mistakes, don't be afraid of nothing, just love, everything and everyone no matter what, what you see in other and you don't like, is a reflect of something that you have to work inside, believe it or not... Just pay attention and you will see. Sometimes it looks horrible, but these is what it is, is someone attitude is bothering you, let's take a look at it, and figure it out what you have to learn about it, and when and how you did the same thing to other or to yourself. You're reflecting in the mirror. Forgive yourself and other and ask for assistance and help if you need it, the

Angels and Archangels will be more than happy to help you. Don't forget that. But you have to ask for help, they can't help if you don't ask for it.

Anytime you decide to take control of your own life, you will know what to do, everyone path is different because anyone is different, different bodies, different minds but we all are one soul, so keep it on mind. I don't want to get into this point. But if you want to know more about it just ask and you will get the information. We are all one, this is amazing, but at the beginning it seems and looks weird, impossible. Don't worry about it; you will realize that sooner or later. As the sun is shining for all of us every day, no matter who we are or where we are, as well God love all of us no matter what. Remember whoever God represent to you, I don't want to do talk about religions; it's not the point now. The point is that no matter who you are, black, white, thin or fat, or whatever the sun is shining for everybody no matter what no matter whom. So enjoy your life, again do baby steps, forgive yourself, and don't give up. Keep doing your inside job, keep smiling, keep breathing, and do everything with love, form the center of you heart. Everything is going to be perfect.

Believe me or not, just try it, or better do it, if it works for you great if not do something else but do anything, don't stay unhappy, unhealthy, and whatever un... you are now. You deserve to be happy, healthy and abundant, do something but do it now.

As you begin to respect yourself, your body, your mind, your soul, you will see everything in another new and fresh perspective, and you will begin the transformation of your entire live. You will take care of your body, with love and kindness, changing some unhealthy habits for others healthier, you will change your sleep, and work and all habits than makes you feel bad. You only have to set your intention to be and feel better with all your heart and you will receive de guidance you need in the process. I'm not going to tell you that it's going to happen in a week, because that's not true, is a long and deep process, but is wonderful, you will feel so blessed, for sure. You just need to enjoy the path, and incorporate some things at the time, and try it and see how you feel, and go on with another thing, you will need to be patient and perseverant, be constant and discipline with your news routines, if you forget something or go back in a bad habit, don't worry, do it again, don't give up. Forgive yourself and move on. I think that the secret is enjoying everything that happens, and you will say what? I can't enjoy this or that... But, just let it go, don't be mad or upset, you will not change it, it happens and that's it, you just have to recognize what was it? Why? And do different next time, you can't do anything else. Don't get stuck in the past it won't help you at all, release the past, and welcome the present with you open heart, mind and soul, and you will be happier every day. As I said before every day is a new beginning, a new life, enjoy it. Smile and breathe... Even if you don't want to smile do it, when you see you image in the mirror smile to yourself always, always, always. A mirror is an opportunity to remind you that you are perfect and beloved, see your face in the mirror and recognize yourself, yes you are perfect, yes you are beautiful or handsome, yes you are definitively perfect. Believe it, and sooner or later you will see it more and more in your life. When you feel tired ask for help, and try a little more, one more step, you almost do it, you are almost there, and be grateful for the new achievement. And if you didn't do it, be graceful too, you only have to do it again, do it different, or do the same with more commitment, with love, be kind with yourself this is great, you will feel great, and if you think that is too good to be true, just do it and you will see.

Another thing I think that is not helpful for our lives is the labeling, everyone wants to put you under a label, I mean she/he is this or that, and put you in some place with a thousand of people's, but it's not nice, we all are unique, our finger print are different from any one else, not even the twins have the same finger print, so why do people and ourselves like to put us I a box with a label?? Nooo!! I began to catch the labeling and was very funny, and then remove it from myself, and then automatically people begin to remove you from labeling. There are a lot of labels, to put a group of person that at some point do the same activity or behavior, you are not that, she o he is weird, is nerd, is good, is bad, is nice, is not nice, and so on, there are millions and more labels and you are not that, you are more and more than a label. You are who you are Period. Think about it. First of all I think that we have to unlabeled ourselves and stop labeling others, eliminate labeling, is super nice when you realize that and you will enjoy the process of un labeling, and as everything else do it with love, with open heart, and everything is going to be more than fine. Use your brain to help you to play this game, it will be so much fun, the brain love to label, lake a machine, and you will change it, be patience and kind with yourself and with other, I know that I said this a thousand of times but you have to be, because if not the process could be painful, and it won't be a pleasure, and it won't be definitive as we deserve it to be.

I have a lot of thing to tell you, but I don't want you to think that how I handle it is the only way, your spiritual path is only yours, and only You will know how to handle it, as the unique human been you are, my purpose writing this book is to help people to open their heart, to help people to remember who they really are, and to help people to be happy, healthier and beloved. To help people to reach their self-love and acceptation and to trust in themselves, I'm not trying to convince you to do this or to do that, I just want you to open your eyes and heart to new opportunities in your own life to see the bigger picture and act in consequence. You have a great opportunity in your live, but it is only your decision, if you want to do the job or if you prefer stay in a comfort zone, without love and compassion for yourself and others. I'd like to explain with more details something's, but I really think that at the end it will be the same but the path will be unique for anyone. That's why I don't want to create false expectation for this or for that, because I'm sure that you will experiment you own cause and effect in all you decisions. I can assure you that you will not be alone, as soon as you decide to work in your internal path, you will receive all the information and insides you will need, your part will be first of all make the decision, second of all work for it and third of all listen to your inner voice, your guidance, and never ever give up. Open your heart and your eyes, to feel and see everything form a new and a magic perspective. Act form your heart with love and not form the ego with fears. There is anything to fear about. Everything is good, is perfect. Surrender and let God guide you, help you and enlighten you entire live.

We all are our own guru, I don't want to repeat myself over and over, but all the answers, all the guidance, all the light, all is inside of you right know, within you, as God says in magical book named Impersonal life, by anonymous. If you have the change read it, you will find some answers, if you are ready to take the next step, and if you have the open heart.

You maybe ask, how can I open my heart? And my answer will be with infinite love, compassion and forgiveness, with yourself fist and then with the others.

Another thing that I think that is important to do is whatever you want to change or incorporate in your live do it at list 21 days, with discipline and been constant, as well it will become an habit as brush your teeth in the morning. Respect yourself if you promise yourself to do something do it, no matter what, and don't do a million of excuses if not, just forgive you and do it the next day, don't feel guilty or depress. It will happen sometimes. More at the beginning, you have to be like the bamboo firm but flexible. Take good care of your internal dialog, catch your thoughts, you are the thinker, the thoughts are not you. You are the one in charge, not your mind, you are the big boss, and you suppose to use your mind as a tool, not your mind using you as a toy, playing games of manipulation, fear and inferiority. Noooooo. You are more than that. You are one within God, as everybody else. You are perfect just on your own way, just as you are Unique. I love this word. Unique, so powerful. I've read a lot of books in My entire life, and I take the message of any of it, if I tell you that I remember in which book a read this of that it's not true, don't be obsess with anything, the response you need you will have it, the message you are waiting for you will have it and you will know for sure what, when and how to do what you need to do in the perfect timing of God not sooner, not later, just in time.

Vulnerability. I'm going to give you the exact definition of vulnerability, from Wikipedia " Main article: Social vulnerability: In its sense, social vulnerability is one dimension of vulnerability to multiple stressors and shocks, including abuse, social exclusion and natural hazards. Social vulnerability refers to the inability of people, organizations, and societies to withstand adverse impacts from multiple stressors to which they are exposed. These impacts are due in part to characteristics inherent in social interactions, institutions, and systems of cultural values." but what I think this is, is when you want to be accepted for others doing thing that you really aren't, I mean kind of chameleon, who change the color with the place it's at, something like that. Trying to pretend to be someone you are not. That's crazy. We must be accepted for who we really are, with all our perfection, a human been, with all our heart. Being spontaneous, and enjoying what we like, and not forcing us to do thing that we don't like, just to be accepted or to avoid judgment and criticism from others. Let's them judge and critics you, the important thing is that it don't have nothing to be with you but others, the only matter you have to worry about is how You feel, and it can sound selfish but is not. Once you realize what you want, what you like, you have to be respectful with yourself honoring your own desires. And you will see a big difference in your mood, you will be without stress and with more happiness, been yourself no matter what, no matter who. The thing is than when you change your behavior, to fit with someone else, you became a sad machine, because you never will want to disappoint anybody, and you want everybody happy, and that's good, but which is the price

you have to pay for that? Your own sadness and
stress, is not fear. Been honest with yourself,
you can be, said and act in the same way no matter
what. And that's the deal, be yourself always this is
awesome. Believe me. People around you is going to
be a little confuse about it because they are used to
see you doing things that you don't want to do, and
when you stop doing that things they will notice. But
don't worry is going to be fine sooner or later they will
figure it out that you are been yourself. And that's a
good thing. You will release yourself and others. Feel
free to be yourself. And they will love you anyway,
because your own love for yourself will shine from
the inside and irradiate this light to everybody who
get in touch with you, and this light and love will
save the world.

Nobody in this world have the power to change
how you feel or make you feel bad, sad, and inferior
or excluded. This exist only in your mind, the only
person that can do it for you is yourself. You are the
only one who aloud this to happen, but if you don't
aloud it, it won't happen again.

Let me tell you again that it's a work to do
step by step, with love and compassion, without

hurries or worries, that won't work. Be patience. Do one thing at the time but be constant and persistent. 21 days without missing one day will be the best way to set the habit in your mind, but if you miss one day, don't worry, continue next day with the commitment that no matter what you will continue. In this work you have to be aware in what you think, what you feel and what you do, been present all the time, and stop the automatic behavior. Doing things and knowing what are you doing or what you don't want to do any more, slow dawn, there is enough time for everything, the time of God is infinite and perfect. If you can take a notebook o an agenda and write how you feel, or what's happening to you daily. It will help a lot, basically to celebrate your achievements and the work well done, and to learn from the experiences that you think o feel uncomfortable, what things you notice that you haven't seen before, and those small details that enlighten your entire life. You will receive messages in different manner, a friend, a book, a radio or TV program, a magazine and so on... As well as listening your inner voice, your thoughts and your feelings. You just have to pay attention at your journey, and everything is going to fit like a puzzle, every part of it is in the right position. You don't have to worry about anything. Whatever you need you already have it. Just ask for help with confidence and with love from your heart and don't be afraid, the fear won't help, you don't have to ignore the fear, you have to face it, and say I'm a beloved child of God and I don't have nothing to fear about, I have faith, I trust and with love all is going to be more than fine. Is important to do affirmation in the beginning because the repetitive and negative thoughts can make us crazy, repeating and repeating over and over... The ego is in its maximum expression. Then when you realize that kind of thoughts you catch it and stop it with a positive though, and repeat it over and over... until the thought of fear disappear. And another thing you must do is treat yourself with love and compassion thoughts, forgive yourself if you do something you don't want to or you don't like to, and learn about the experience and know that if it happens is because you have something to learn about it, something to work about it, and you will know what it's sooner or later. I know that you must be thinking that I'm crazy, that's fine, I use to think the same with some authors of some of the many many books I read, but at the end I realize that all that guys was right. And you will realize it too, sooner or later... I'm sure of that, it happens to me. I use to think is too difficult I can't do this or that, but that's not true, nothing is too difficult and we can do anything we desire with our heart, with love and to share with others, to save us and others, to have a deep connection with ourselves, with others and with Mother Earth our home, our house. By the way we have to take care of Mother Earth, in small things at the time, but doing something. You will figure it out, which will be your contribution to these work with Mother Earth, every one of us have to do their part, small o big things but doing something.

I know that is a lot of information, I know that you can be confuse, is completely normal, read it take that part that you think o feel that can help you and practice it, do it, and again one step at the time, and baby steps, with love and commitment. At the end this is your live and only you know what to do, when, and how. You only have to hear your inner lovely voice and put in mute the external noise and the ego internal voice, you will know when the internal voice is your inner voice and when is the voice of the ego, first of all you inner voice is a lovely whisper who looks like your own voice sometimes, and only give you advices and instructions to do things with love and compassion, thinking in all the people and not only in yourself, and the voice of the ego, always want a confrontation, is a selfish voice, is a laud voice, that always seems angry, despair, and have always fear to something or someone, always want to heart you or others, wants to make you feel guilty, sad, inferior, and you definitively are none of this, so make that voice to be quiet with love and compassion. As you can see the keys are LOVE AND COMPASSION. And those keys open all doors in the spiritual and in the material world; you will see love and compassion in everywhere. As much as you treat yourself and others with love and compassion, as much you will be treated with love and compassion. And you don't have to do that just for the outcome of receiving but if you do it with all your heart it will happens to you sooner or later. And you will notice it, you will enjoy your live and every step in your way, been present and felling connect with the energy of

God, felling beloved and loving everything and everyone.

Your life is going to change 360 grades and you will incorporate in your daily life, new and divine activities that will fulfill all your needs. I don't like to talk about needs, because we really don't need anything you have everything everyone have everything but we don't remember. This is our work. To remember who we are and ask for our divine heritage. We are a soul living in a human body, and this human body is your temple, you have to take care of it, and when you begin to listen to your inner voice, your will realize what your body is asking for, what is a food that is appropriate for your body your mind and spirit, and will help you in the realization of your higher self. You are a channel of the Divine, a channel of light and love, and you will feel it, you will share it with everyone in your way, because when you are working with this magnitude of light and love you will be more than happy to share it with others.

To begin the path of discover yourself, in my opinion the first step you will have to take, must be grateful for everything you get, first in the morning and last at night, everyday all days. Do a pray with your own words or your favorite pray to ask for spiritual guidance and help in your journey.

Second of all must be stay alone, quiet and in silence for a while every day. Some of us don't know how to be alone, we have to be with someone else or with the cellphone, the iPad, the computer and so on, we are not use to be quiet and alone, but we have to remember how to do it, be with you few minutes every day, all days. And you will begin to hear you inner voice. This is what some people call meditation. But the first time you listen the word meditation you'll fill nervous, you'll think I can't do this, this is for illuminated people, but it is not, and it is for everyone who wants to remember how to listen their inner voice. The voice of God within you. The Angels and Archangels will be happy to help you if you ask for help; they have to respect your free will. As soon as you ask you will get it, anything you want if is mean to be for your higher self. Sometimes we don't get what we ask for, because we don't really know what we want sometimes, and sometimes is not the appropriate moment to get it or is not mean to be for your higher self. Everything happens in the perfect timing. As I said before it is like a rally, once you accomplish one goal, you will receive the instructions to the next one, is a work of all days, there are no holidays in the spiritual path, is a work of 24X7 and your outcome will be joy, love, compassion, happiness and abundance, and all the gifts of God, of the spiritual path, your own realization.

I know that it looks complicated and difficult but is not, you only have to do it, a little bit each day, if it works for you great, if not, try anything else but do something to enlighten your life and be happy, healthy and abundant. I just can tell you that three years ago I was just like you, lost, unhappy, fat and sad. But now I do my job every day and I feel beloved, happy, healthy, and abundant. I have to tell you that some days I feel uncomfortable but I just take a deep breath and let it go, and look around to see why it happen, what I miss and I always knew it. And I feel grateful for the opportunity of known myself a little more, and to go back into my path with love and compassion. Be honest with yourself and with others in any situation. I know that is easier to say little lies sometimes but I can assure you that you will fill better, if you assume your responsibility and tell the truth, you will be vulnerable in front of others but you will be extremely peaceful, is a commitment with yourself you have to catch yourself in this little lies and fix it and think about it and know for sure that been honest is the best way ever. The others will notice it and is very uncomfortable, to think and feel something and express another. It create a dissociation inside of you that other people can perceive and it will make you feel depress and sad trying to express something that is not you, is not your true, is not your deep feeling, is not your essence. So the easy way is to be honest anytime no matter what. You don't need to be rude, to be honest and sincere, you may talk from the button of your heart, everything you do in that way is going to be fine, you can't be wrong talking from your heart, because it's your Divine guidance, your higher self talking to you, through you, and the results only can be lovely.

When you begin the process of take care of yourself and take control of your own life, you will have to make conscious decisions, we all do decisions every time, every day, but when we make it in automatic, the results sometimes don't like us.

Perhaps, when you are present and make your own decisions, you always have the opportunity to know if it's o it isn't what you want, and do it again in a different way, both ways are fine, because you did it because you thought that is was the best for you at the moment. And it was, so don't worry, just keep yourself present in your own life, and enjoy the magical path that is awaiting for you. When I first began my inner work, I swear it was hard, because I was completely focus outside of me. In others, basically. And I was really depress, as much as I thought I was bipolar, I'm not, by the way. But the ups and downs in my mood was a constant in my life, because my mood depended on someone else, if they like my clothes, my speaking, my hair, my friends, my behavior, it was really horrible, give anyone outside of you the power to change you mood, it's insane, for real. If someone told me not to do that, because I don't like to, I didn't do it, even if I do like it, If someone told me I don't like how you look with this pants, I change immediately, even if I do like my pants, and so on... my self-esteem was poor those days, I always obey to the others desires, even if I wasn't agree with it, I never ever said no, never ever... And I was pretty unhappy those days. Then when I lost my 19 years job and I realize who my real friends are, just a few, I began my journey to a new an wonderful life guide by the Divine. As I told you before, this is not going to happen reading this book if you don't do you inner work, and is not going to happens in one day, it's not a one day work and it's a journey that you have to decide to take with all your been, it's a commitment with yourself and it's a commitment with your higher self. You will have, as a said before, as help as you ask for. I had it and I still have it. So you will. The ball is on your side, it's up to you.

When we are living the automatic live, our thoughts are, why this is happening to me? why they do this to me? why, why, and why? But the thing is that the question is not why the others do that to me, the question is why I allow them to do this to me? That is the question, it's not about the others, it's about you, and only you can change it, only you can work with it, only You! Nobody else have the power to influence your life If you don't let them do it, nobody else can't do something to you if you don't let them do it, it's only up to you, and you have to take responsibility for your acts, and the effect of your actions. If you don't like what you see, change the the inputs in your life and the outcome will change as an effect of your acts. It's cause and effect. If you want to enjoy your life in a different way, you have to act in a different way. It looks like impossible, but it's not at all, is difficult? It's not, is easy? It's not, it just IS. Is your life and your journey, your own path... Only you have the power to change it. The decision is on you. If I did it any one else can do it... So, make possible for you a life full of joy, happiness, abundance and all the good things that you deserve and are yours for divine inheritance. The other thing is that if you don't do the decisions and begin procrastinating the universe will do it for you, and you won't like it. I won't. I procrastinated my decisions as much as I could, but at the end when the universe make it form me, was hard, I had to begin since the fist step. Like a baby. But I can tell you my friend, now I love it, I turned back and I understand so many things now, that I even imagine before, I'm grateful with the universe for make me stop procrastinating in my own life, it's the best thing that had happen to me ever. And I'm still working on it, every single day. I really enjoy it. I'm not depress any more, I'm definitively not bipolar, I have new healthy habits, I quit bad habits and addictions, and I feel very very good know. I have a new and wonderful life, I love me, and I love everybody else. Thanks God... Love you!

I don't know what else to say, I don't want to repeat myself over and over, I know that if I'm writing these book, and you are reading it, is because, some of the information about how I'm doing the shift or the big change in my life, can help someone else in their own path, because I got and still get a lot of help from different books, I was guided too, in un expectable ways. You will know. Be patience. Don't get anxious, breath an smile. Everyday you will learn a little bit more. And you will feel better and better each single day. Live you present time as the last one, because that's the only thing we have. The present time. The past is not there anymore and the future in uncertain, no one know what's going to happen tomorrow. So better do your best every second of you present and you will guarantee, that you will be more than happy. Without expectations, we have a lot of expectations in a lot of different things, and that make us extremely unhappy because we want things happens in some way and them it doesn't happens as we want, we get mad, and so on, with us an with others, when we have high expectations in someone else and we don't get what we expect to get, we're upset with the others, but is not their fault is yours. You put your expectation on them and they don't even know, and they don't care. So, don't do that. Just ask honestly and directly what you want, and if they can do that. And that's it, simplify your life, if the can good, and if they can't good too. It's your business is not theirs. It's the same when someone else have an expectation on you, and you don't even know, you do what you want to do, if they like it good, and if not good, is not your business agin, it's theirs. It looks a little confuse but the point is that living your life with expectations is so stressful, better be honest, ask, and set an intention not an expectation.

Another thing that I think is very important is don't take things personal, everyone in their head have an entire world, and sometimes we don't even realize it, if we answer in a different tone, or if we see or don't see someone, if we take a call or not, everybody is in their own business, if I call you and you don't answer is fine, you must be busy, we use to think She or he don't want to talk with me, she must be angry with me, I must do something wrong and so on... And it's not true, because maybe the other person was just busy, and we do a big drama in our head, then when the other person call you back you are already upset, that's crazy, and they even realize that. Don't take anything personal. It's not about you but the others, every one have a million things on mind at the time, don't worry, things will happen at the perfect time. Some people are not living in the present time, are distract or just busy, as you too, sometimes, so let it go, smile, breath and think it's not about me, he o she is in his or her own world. Let it be. You do your best to be present and pay attention in what you are doing, do it with all your senses, you have to train yourself to do that, it's easy do one thing at a time, and do it good, the best you can, with love, whatever it is, when you finish these one go to the other, don't disperse your energy in a thousand of unfinished things at the time, you will be tired, with low energy and with a thousand things to finish. Remember the only thing you have to do is be happy, smile and take a deep breath, no matter what. Sometimes we feel exhausted and don't want to do anything, and that's fine just, don't do that like an habit, because sometimes is the ego trying to push you out of your own path, and sometimes is the ego trying to make you do things in a hurry because of the fear. You will know when you really need to be quiet and let the things just happens or when to act, it'll be always a lovely advise, not an order to obey, basically, this is going to be the difference. You will feel it, deep in your heart. I've to tel you that is a little confuse sometimes, because always the ego speak louder and have a sense of urgency and that can scare you in the beginning, because you can say if I don't do that something bad is going to happen to me and this is the ego trying to manipulate you with this drama, don't let it happens. If you feel the urgency to do something is going to be because you will help someone else or because you will improve the quality of your life. Actually it's going to be because you will be happier or you will make others happier. Ego have a lot of tricks to let you down, but we will remember how to stop it. Basically do all things with love and compassion and you will be more than fine. I know that all that stuff sounds a little complicated, but at the end it's not complicated at all. You will see for sure. I would like see you taking control of your life and making your own decisions with love and I swear that your entire life will change. Is not necessary to be rude with the others, because they will become upset sometimes because you are the center of your life and not they any more, you will change your centers of attention from the outside to your inside, and some things are not going to be so important as it was before, and some people too, and they will notice that, and will try to manipulate you, and try to make you get back to your past life, but it's not going to happen. Just make your point clear and they have two options accept you like you really are or not, but again is not you business is theirs. Your business is yourself and their business are theirselves, if anyone change the center of their life to the inside of their hearts, the world will be transform to a peaceful place for everybody. I'm not telling you that you have to become a hermit, or selfish, I'm telling you that you have to remember and enjoy who you really are by yourself and for that you must be alone for a while, and then you can enjoy and share with others from a new conscious of love and compassion, and it will be awesome. I have to tell you that you will need to be focus in what you want and keep it on your heart because you will have to take a lot of tests to prove that it's what you want, some subtle and repetitive, just to make sure that you know that it's what you want, it's funny. Now I can smile about that but in the beginning I could not understand what was it about and why, the trials will stop when you feel comfortable with your decisions and have the courage to support it no matter what. And sometimes you will be test again just in case, it sound funny to me now, and I know that you must be thinking I don't know how to do this or that, but I'm sure that you will figure it out, as I did. You will have assistance, just ask for help with your heart open and you will get it.

One of the most important thing that I realized was to know myself, to hear my inner voice and to treat myself like a princess, enjoying to be with myself alone, and to hear my body, our bodies give us a lot of signals, but we don't listen, sometimes the signals are about food, that don't make us feel well, others are about rest a little more, to relax, other to quit addictions and bad habits that make us feel sick, and sometimes just take control of our thoughts. To hear this signals we have to be aware, and we have to silence the noise and hear our lovely inner voice, the noise could be internal or external, our own thoughts or the tv, the computer, cellphone, friends, alcohol, junk food, etc... Step by step you will fell the desire to purify your live in all senses, your food physical or intellectual. What programs you see on tv, or what kind of lectures do you do, what is the quality of your thoughts, your closer people, do you take care of your body, with healthy food and some exercise, do you take time to relax and enough sleep hours? How often do you do things that you love? How often do you smile? Do you have an addition to scape from your reality? All this is going to change, as soon as you make the decision to allow God to guide you on your real path, to help you to remember, who you really are. As soon as you open your heart and decide to love you and take good care of yourself, it's a decision that only you can make, and as said before you will receive help as soon as you ask for, with an open heart, with faith, certain and with love and compassion.

I'm trying not to repeat myself over and over, but it's all connected, one thing come to the other, there is a sequence of activities, everything is going to happen in the perfect time, and you have to make your own decision and it's going to happen when you are ready, just you will know when is your perfect time, for everything in your life. You must have to rebuilt your own life since the ground, star over with God within you. And rebirth in a new life full of blessings, joy, happiness, health, wealth and... love and compassion. That's what we deserve and that's what we have now and will have forever as our inheritance of our God father.

Look the abundance of the nature, is perfect, I haven't seen a bird stress out, for food or money ever. The nature is perfect and have the certain that every thing is going to be fine, all their needs are going to be satisfy and fulfill because our father care about us and about everything on earth, as equals, there are no levels for God, there is no good or bad, we are all the same, part of God, one within God, and one within the Mother Earth. And so it's. We just have to let it go and let it God, as Doreen's said. The Universe is perfect and we are part of it. That's why we are perfect too. We have to work with our sense of separation because there is not separation between us and God, us and the Universe, us and Mother Earth, we are all part of God within. It looks complicated but it's not. As I said before. You will figure it out. Sooner o later. Every thing is up to You, and you have the right, the power and the strength to take control of your live and surrender... Let God guide You, remember who you are. You are a beloved child of God.

When you realize that you have to do some changes in you life because you want to and not because someone else want to, you will gain self respect. This is the beginning of your new life, to remember who you really are and to know yourself more than anyone else. Become your best friend, take care of you, and provide yourself with confidence and strength. You will rebirth in a brand new life, full of blessings, love, compassion and you will feel better and better every day, and depressions, addictions, unhappiness, etc., will go far away of you. You'll have to forgive your self and others one and a million times, as much as you need it, as much asYou release the pain, we are in pain for many things, because we aloud it, from ourselves or from others, and this is a pain in our heart, that feels so real, but is not. As soon as you forgive and let it go, you will heal your heart, is not easy at all, but you don't have to denied the grief, you have to accept it, know that if it is there is because you aloud it, and you can heal it. It's not about anyone else. Is about you, yes again. Because nobody can hurt you, unless you aloud it. And I'm not talking about physical hurt, I'm talking about this pain in your soul in your heart, deep inside on you, that makes you tears just when you remember it. This hard times when we didn't have control of our live and emotions, and you aloud others, usually your loved ones to treat you in an in appropriated way, because you love them, and maybe you think that they do this or those things because of that, but it's not true. Nobody can treat you as a slave, or as an inferior been or like you don't deserve this or that, or like you are their property and they can't treat you as they want, no no no no.... Sometimes we aloud it because we don't want to loose this loved ones or because we feel vulnerable and we don't want to show who we really are because we don't want to be judge or we don't want them to be mad on us, my friend... I can tell you than non of this is going to work, this persons are not going to change your real essence and you an they will notice that its not working at all, must of people wants to change the way you are, but the only one that can make that decision is You, nobody else can even imagine to change you, they can try, but is not going to happen, well nor permanently. And if you do so, you will feel so bad inside, like a division inside of you. Like two different persons inside of you, and this hurts, this make you tears, because you are not been honest with yourself or with others, and they feel it, as a lier, and you really are not a lier, you're just trying to make them happy being unhappy, and in this way, trust me all of you are going to be unhappy. As I said before, I guess, you must focus your attention in yourself first and you have to synchronize you heart, your thought, and your feeling, all of this must be in the same direction because if not, you will look as dishonest, and you're not, but you looks like, because you think something, but you feel another thing and in the inside of your heart you know that is another one, this is heavy talking my friend. Sometimes this disconnection comes trying to make everybody happy but you can't. Unfortunately you can't make anybody happy. You only can't make yourself happy. As well you happiness or unhappiness don't depends on anyone else but you. It's hard to me to explain this, because this was the most difficult issue for me, but finally I realize with my inner work that this happens for a reason, and it makes you stronger, and not stronger like a steel woman, because I'm not, stronger because you know yourself more than anybody and you love yourself more than anybody, and you can deal with older situations and see it in a different perspective that don't affect your feelings, because as I said before is not personal, it's not about you, it's about the other person trying to get the old you back, with manipulation, and all that stuff than break you down before, but now is not working. Because you love them but you love you more, and you care about them, but you care about you more, and you will not accept or aloud nothing that don't match with you and your higher self, and who you really are. Of course with love and compassion, everybody have their own path, and you are or were part of their path as they are or were part of yours, sometimes they were there to teach you something, and sometimes you were there for teach them something, as soon as everybody learn their lesson or what they need to learn or remember, the situation disappear and both of you will see things in a different way. It's not easy to me to explain it, but you will figure it out by yourself I'm sure of that. I think that this is going to be a book that you can read once and again, and as soon as you realize somethings you will be able to continue with the next step, I'm doing it with my heart because I feel that some people around the world can't be in a situation I was few year ago, when I thought that there were no light at the end of the tunnel, and I was drowning myself in a glass if water, with a limit perspective of live. And when I turn around my eyes to heaven all my perspective change, because I was looking my answers in the wrong place. All the answers you need you will find it inside of you, you have to silence the outside noise and hear your inner voice, and you will clearly see that you are the light at the end of the tunnel. Your light is inside of you, you have the power to change your own life and help others, in the way. Don't judge, don't take anything personal, be kind, and know that we all are one, all of us, I know that it looks unbelievable, but It's what it is. Remember love and compassion, with every one. Smile and breath. Enjoy every second of your life like the last one, every sunrise, every sunset, the clouds, the birds, the flowers, the rain, the snow, enjoy everything, all things are gifts that you have every day, look to the horizon don't look down, it makes you feel worried, desperate, it don't aloud you to enjoy the marvelous gifts that we receive from Mother Earth every day, the small things that can change your mood and your thoughts, your entire live. The small things that matters. Beautiful things, you will be surprised yourself with all the small gifts, all the details, You only need to be present and in the present time, let go the past, work in your present with all your heart, without expectations, and you will be guide with divine love and divine light. Don't be afraid, you are always protect, your guardian Angel is always with you, ask for help, company, advice or what ever you need and you will get it, the Angels and Archangels will be more than happy to help you, you only have to call upon them and they will assist you. Have faith and confidence, and the certain that every thing you need or desire you will get it, or something better for you, in the perfect timing. Don't worry about the time, it's unlimited and perfect. Don't worry about the supplies you will have all you need, basically don't worry at all. Is not necessary and you are not going to solve anything being worried about it. Just let it go and let it God. What's the worst thing that could happen to us? Die? Everybody is going to die, sooner o later, so be happy an enjoy every second as the last one, smile and breath. Remember you are more than a body. Much much more. Take good care of your body, that's important, cook your meals with love, choose the best products, take enough rest and avoid process food, artificial drinks, alcohol, sodas, excess of sugar, salt, wheat, enjoy your meal without any distraction reserve this time just for your meal, every thing can wait 10 or 15 minutes, chew the foods well, our stomach don't have teethes, take a little nap 10 minutes is enough. You deserve a quiet meal. I would like to say go vegan, but it's up to you, your body will advise what food is better for you, and you will consider avoid some kind of food, you will purify your body and you will have to do the same with your mind and feelings. Is a process, remember baby steps, no rush, take your time.

Well... I don't not what else to tell you, I thinks you have a lot of work to do, but is going to be a pleasant work, for your spiritual, physical, and mental growth, the best work you have ever imagine, a work for you and within you, it'll be a amazing journey, you will see. I hope this book helps you to improve the quality of your life, and helps you to be happier, healthier, and deepen your connection with your inner voice, as I said before, everyone have their own way to do their thing, because everyone is unique, that why I don't do a lot of details, because you will get better results if you do it at your own way, and taking some guidance and advice from others, like me o anyone else that you feel guide to contact, remember the spiritual guidance is available for you, as soon as you ask for it, so don't procrastinate and begin your inner work now, no more excuses, you can do it, you will see, you desire a better life you will have it for sure. And you and all around you will shine with divine light.

Sometimes you will feel lonely, and maybe sad, but it's because you don't know you yet, it's a new beginning for you, remember that you have to realize who you really are, you have to release all these old believes, and discover which believes make you happy, which is your real essence, what you like or dislike, all about You, your own rebirth, and them you will adapt these new you to your reality, your life and you will do the necessary changes to be consistent in mind, heart and feelings. Only one direction for all you. Only one speech only one, the one that will support you and the one that will make you growth in you spiritual path. And will aloud you to let behind all your fears and be sure that you are a holly child of God. You have to be persistent and don't give up, I'm not telling you that is going to happen from today to tomorrow, because is not true, is a process as I told you before, and you can do it. Step by step, with confidence and faith in yourself and in you higher self. Breath, smile and go on and on.

Well they insist in the details. Ok, first you have to work in the priorities in your life, leave the attachments to the material things, as soon as you leave it away, you will have more, if not you will loose it all, literally, in order to remember that you are not your belonging you are more more than that, and nothing material can make you happy for ever, listen carefully, it could be as easy as you realize that, and change the focus of your attention in the spiritual path, and the material things will flow in your direction and won't run away from you. We deserve to be be wealthy, and we are, but we don't recognize the source of the abundance, we are looking in the wrong place and for the wrong reasons. We must remember that the God within us, is the source of all abundance, and we are the owners of our destiny, we build our life as we want to, with our thoughts, with our actions, we are the constructors of our life, so if you see in your life something that you don't like, is because you created it, and only you can change it. Enlighten your thoughts and take control of you mind, your mind suppose to serve you in your purpose, not you been a server of you mind. You have to use your mind in a positive way to create the life you deserve and you are able to live. We are a creators as our creator is, we are part of the creator and we can do all things that the creator does, but we need to remember that and work in consequence. In my opinion we have to relax and let God guide us, surrender. I'm going to explain why I said remember instead of learn, and it's because we already know every thing, but we forgot it, and that's part of our Divine plan, to recognize ourselves as spiritual being living a human experience. And we have to remember and work by ourselves in our spiritual path, of course with all the help and guidance you'll need, as soon as you ask for it.

You will feel afraid or alone sometimes, but this is a challenge to discover how much have you learn or remember about who you are, you don't have nothing to worry about and you are never alone, you are part of the Divine live, part of the Mother Earth, you have all inside of you, you are always in the best company you can have. Enjoy your live, just be present and be happy, healthy and wealthy. Smile and breath. You have all you need or desire. Every thing is in you, is within you, because you are part of the Divine, God, the Holy Spirit or whatever you what to name it, all is the same. The same energy of love and compassion, abundance and gratitude, divine light and guidance. We are all one. We all are part of all and all is part of us.

It's all about love, everyone wants to be love, but the first thing you have to do is love yourself, that's the greatest love of all, then you can appreciate other love, in all different kinds of, love is in the air... Love yourself and you will attract people who will love themselves and you. This is so beautiful. Like the energy you feel in Christmas, everybody wants to share, everybody have love and compassion for the other, the magic of Christmas that you have to represent all days of your live, to yourself first and them automatically with other because you will realize that we are all one. It is amazing. Isn't it? Give a touch of Christmas to you live and all the universe will conspire with you to realize your dream, the magic of love and compassion...

When you feel good with yourself every place in the world is home. Actually home is inside of you, enjoy your own company, and then you will love to share your gift with others. Be happy, be yourself, discover yourself, and who you are, and what you want, listen to your inner voice. The voice of God within you. I'd like to tell you a lot of things but the real thing is that you have to discover it by yourself. That's the true, I can write millions of pages, thousands of books, to explain you how life works, but the real thing is that only you will know, how life works for you, every one is unique, and every one have their own manner to discover their own path, I just need to tell you that, and tell you that you are not alone, you have a lot of help, just ask for it and you will get it. This is a wonderful place and if sometimes you think and feel that is not fair, probably it is not, but it has a purpose, every thing have a reason to be, good o bad in the moment is all for good at the end, it teach you something, and it has an ultimate and greatest purpose. I've never been so happy in my entire life, and I have been very unhappy most of the time in my life, worrying for insignificant things, and expecting to find happiness outside of me. Now I know that the most beautiful things in the world are free and the most beautiful love that you can find in your live is inside of you, is loving yourself and being grateful with all things and with everyone, no matter what. Nothing is permanent in the material world, and everything is permanent in the spiritual world, you only have to remember how to balance both.

Remember the joy in the small things that the universe give us all days, and be thankful for be alive and for the gift of the human been, the gift of life. Even if you don't know yet how it's a gift you will realize It sooner or later, open your heart, and listen. Listen to your inner voice, your intuition the you inside of you, the spirit inside of your body, the best part of you. It's amazing. It's all joy, happiness and hope. Even when you cry is a beautiful thing, even when you smile... Love is in the air, is the energy of God is the best thing ever, even when you are alone and sad, think about love and you will smile, love yourself, it's the best way to love others, with all your heart.

Recommend books

A COURSE IN MIRACLES ACIM By
Foundation for inner peace

IMPERSONAL LIFE BY ANONYMOUS

THE ANGEL THERAPY HANDBOOK by
Doreen Virtue